Metastatic Madness

Metastatic Madness

How I Coped With a Stage 4 Cancer Diagnosis

Carol A. Miele

To order additional copies of this book, contact:
Xlibris Corporation
1-888-795-4274
www.Xlibris.com
Orders@Xlibris.com
121596

Contents

Dedication

- This book and its collection of poems are dedicated to Paula Ronjon, MD, my Oncologist at the Henry Cancer Center, Geisinger Medical Center, Wilkes Barre, Pennsylvania. She competently managed my care since diagnosis and handed my life back to me so I could enjoy the time I have left with my family and friends.
I am eternally grateful.

- I want to honor my parents, Angelo and Mary Bruno. My father suffered from advanced gastric cancer that was not treatable, but he handled it with the strength and indomitable spirit we had seen tested many times over the years.

- My mother had many setbacks in her life and was often ill, but she was always a sweet, nurturing and loving mother who never had a harsh word for anyone. As she lay dying with barely enough breath in her lungs to speak, she softly spoke her last words to me, 'I love you'. I felt so comforted hearing them. Even in death, her last thoughts were for others.

- Their lives were a struggle, he worked as a coal miner for many years and she sewed blouses in a local factory. They had so little in life. Towards the end, my father said somewhat wistfully, "Mary, things were just starting to look up for us."

- This dedication would be incomplete without mentioning a great source of my inspiration and will to live . . . my family, especially my grandchildren Joey, Emily and Alex.

Acknowledgements

I am fortunate to have had supporters along the way to encourage me to write and to publish this book. My husband, Gene, who is my caregiver, my partner, my love, and always honest in his opinions. He told me after reading through my poems 'they're good.' And that was good enough for me. Many thanks to my daughter, Marisa Miele Grier, who has been astute in pointing out spelling or grammatical errors, and suggesting ideas about the poems that were insightful and useful. She would read one of my poems and immediately spot a phrase that could be worded better. My younger daughter, Kristen Miele Beatty, was supportive of my 'creative efforts' and was always there for me. She presented me with a '*Wonder Woman*' *Snuggie* to wear at my very first chemo treatment so I would be strong! She was there for my Oncology visits, even some chemotherapy visits. She took notes and questioned anything that wasn't completely clear, teaching me the value of critical thinking. I have collaborated with both daughters on past projects. This one is near and dear to my heart.

I gratefully acknowledge the valuable editorial assistance that I received from my sister Dee and her husband Andrew Gillow. Great fans of poetry, they were delighted to read each poem and other contents of the book. Their reliability and consistency were paramount to completion of this manuscript. I am grateful to my lifelong friend Yvonne Panfili and new online friend Jeanie Turner who suggested that I publish my poems. Also, my online friend Pam Breakey, who suggested early on that I copyright my poems. I would like to acknowledge my cousins Karen Fairweather and Nancy Embrico, along with my sister-in-law, Catherine Miele, for their continuous support and encouragement. Many thanks to my Oncologist, Dr. Paula Ronjon, who gave me her unconditional approval when she said, "I like everything you write" and nurses at the Cancer Center whose feedback inspired me to continue writing. Finally, I would be remiss not to mention my closest companion, Flora, who was literally at my feet as

I wrote this book. She lay on her dog bed under my computer desk and continued her vigil as long as I continued writing.

The women on *bcmets.org* who have Metastatic Breast Cancer also inspired me to write these poems. I read their stories and plights in their online posts, referencing their perils in some oblique way as I sympathize with their struggles. They are my '*Metster Sisters & Brothers*' who comprise a worldwide network of hearts and souls. We provide each other strength through daily advice, helpful tips, cyber hugs, and grief, when one of us is lost to this miserable disease. The usual outcry is, "Cancer sucks!" I couldn't have said it better.

Every cancer patient I have met, talked with, or taken care of during my 45 year career as a professional nurse has in some way prepared me for this and showed me how to be brave. Cancer tends to give you a new perspective on life. You prioritize things differently. You may want to see the world, or you want more quality time with your loved ones. I wanted to do both. Gene and I took that long awaited trip to Italy this past year to celebrate our 35th wedding anniversary. I know we may not see our 50th, or even our 40th, but we sure celebrated this one. *Arrivederci!*

Foreword

Some will say the value of poetry is its aesthetic expression, timeless thoughts, unusual insights and penetrating meaning. Hopefully, this book brings these qualities to the reader. My intent is to inform and assist those struggling with a metastatic cancer diagnosis, whether their own, a family member or close friend.

The poems are about my experience with a first time diagnosis of cancer and the shocking fact that I was already Stage 4 . . . I thought the previous negative test results meant that I was home free. Welcome to *Cancer Land*!

My poems began as a catharsis. I felt better when I wrote my thoughts on paper. Those thoughts resulted in a book that's a window to my soul. It's my wish that all people with cancer have peace, love, supportive family and friends, super physicians, and a life force that rises above anything cancer does to bring you down.

Introduction

Looking back at my early experience with Stage 4 Breast Cancer, I have identified at least five phases I transitioned through while learning to cope with my diagnosis:

Shock and Awe

Betrayal and Despair

Loneliness and Loathing

Complying and Compensating

Adapting and Advocating

These five phases are groups of feelings and reactions that came in waves. Some overlapped and even recurred on occasion. It's a little like the ebb and flow of the ocean's tides. One minute I would be feeling fine and getting through my day. Then, a moment later, I would feel this wave of emotion wash over me. It would generally reduce me to tears. I would think about losing my family and having a prognosis that predicts my life will be cut much shorter than I had hoped. As I experienced it, each phase gradually dissipated to be taken over by another less debilitating phase; until you finally feel strong and in control intellectually and stable emotionally. I believe it's all part of the healing process. Hopefully, you can avoid getting stuck in one of the early phases. If that occurs, your progress can be greatly hampered. You must be prepared for disappointments, delays, long waits, uncomfortable or painful tests and treatments all along the way. If you can't get past the fear or anger in the earliest phase, you may not be able to manage your illness or its accompanying issues very effectively.

These phases of coping are essential to your mental and emotional well-being. You need to be able to express how you feel, and not bottle it all up inside. You need to grieve and to feel sad. Then you need to find ways to move on. You will need some supports in place to do this. This can be provided by your family, close friends, a volunteer or Social Worker, a Chaplain or Minister, even another cancer patient. This means having someone to talk to, to confide in, to help you with your daily chores and activities of living, getting groceries or medications, or simply running errands. It would be good for you to have someone accompany you to each Oncology visit, and hopefully for Chemotherapy treatments as well. You may not feel much like driving after an infusion. In some cases, medications are given before or during the infusion that can make you feel very sleepy. Driving would be prohibited in this case. You would benefit from having someone take notes during your visits as you will be unlikely to remember what is said afterwards. My younger daughter did this for me. I remember reading the notes afterwards and thinking, "I don't remember that being discussed", or "I forgot all about that new medication I'm going on next week; good thing it's in the notes!" You are still likely in a state of shock in the earliest phase, your mind can't take it all in because its already saturated with fear and worries.

You will eventually find ways of coping as you go through each phase so that you can focus all your energy on healing. We all deal with these situations a little differently, but no one walks out of the oncology office after being diagnosed with metastatic cancer and not feel the earth suddenly shift under your feet; or have the sensation that the floor has been yanked out, leaving your feet dangling in air. Its likely you'll feel you're in a state of imbalance, not only emotionally and mentally, but physically as well, for at least a brief period of time. If not, it's because you're numb from the shock. It could last seconds, maybe hours, and, for some, its days. The important thing is to regain your footing and move on!

For me, I felt like I was walking through a long tunnel and I couldn't see or hear very well because I was frightened. I was paralyzed by fear. All I could think about was that I was going to die . . . the notion of being able to go on with my life didn't come until later, when I began to adapt and cope better. That was when I finally realized that '*Death*' wasn't even remotely ready for me. Looking back, I can tell you; when you're filled with fear, it's hard to do anything. You're reluctant to make any decisions. You want them made for you. You don't want to think about the future. You don't think you have one. You don't want small talk, chit chat, social occasions, or any kind of get together. This is a serious matter and it requires all your energy and attention.

Its also very easy to panic when you've hit Stage 4, because you are essentially at the end of the line. Beyond you is the '*Great Beyond*'. You seriously need to keep your perspective and your head squarely on your shoulders. But it can be mind-bending. It can make you a sinner or a saint. It can numb you or it can spur you into action. It all depends on your mind set, your life experiences and those around you. Do you have a supportive family and friends, or are you winging this on your own? Is your Oncologist a compassionate communicator, or did you have this diagnosis laid out for you like a slab of meat on a cold marble counter? A lot of how you handle it is perception.

While you are grieving over this fatal diagnosis, the fluffy aspects of life are not only meaningless, but it can really tick you off! Beware well-meaning neighbors who bring their newborn grandchild in to 'cheer you up'. It will only remind you that you will not be around to see your grandchildren grow up. Before long, you realize your new cancer diagnosis isn't really good company. In fact, its downright boring and drags you down. You've had enough of being alone, alternately weeping and sobbing, being morose, and withdrawing into yourself. So, how do you bust out?? Well, I started by creating a '*circle of support*'. I read in a booklet about cancer that it's important to surround yourself with positive people, as they give off positive energy. It makes sense! and it's what you really need at this phase. You don't need a bunch of '*crepe hangers*' around you. I contacted a group of women I felt close to and had a positive relationship with to form this *circle of support*: my grown daughters, my sister, my sister-in-law, a cousin whose mother had metastatic breast cancer, a cousin who is a breast cancer survivor, a lifelong friend and a former co-worker.

I asked them if they would be my 'inner circle', that I would keep them informed of my progress or lack of progress by e-mail. I updated them after each treatment and told them how it went, how I was feeling and any problem areas. It was great! They often sent encouraging messages or inquired about things they wanted to know more about. Some even sent me articles they researched that were helpful. When one of them called, it was easier to talk about my cancer as they were on the same page as me. They already knew what was going on so we could take it from there. There were no taboos or hesitations, no 'elephant in the room'. I felt so lucky to have these women pulling for me. I could almost feel their positive energy seeping into my body and raising me up so I could get on with my life. Another benefit is that you can print out these updates and save them as a record of your treatment history.

When I began losing my hair, my younger daughter brought me several scarves and showed me how to create attractive head coverings to disguise my new baldness. She even created a brochure with photos she took of herself wearing various head wrap styles. She's a professional artist and very creative. The brochure was quite helpful, you know, 'a picture is worth a thousand words'! When the time came, she gave me a buzz cut to get rid of the thinning hair that was coming out of my comb in clumps and no longer worthy of a brush. I had a mix of hats, scarves, wigs and knit caps to cover my bald head and maintain warmth as well as my self confidence.

Your head gets pretty darn cold when there's nothing covering it, especially the back of your neck. I wore a lot of turtlenecks and 'hoodies' throughout the cold winter months as I was going through chemo. She also brought me a 'brow kit' when my eyebrows disappeared. It was effective and easy to use. There were two powders to replicate my natural shade, a few templates so I could pick the shape and thickness of brow I'm most comfortable with. I attended a *Look Good, Feel Better* program provided by the American Cancer Society and really enjoyed learning more about improving my wan looks. I even learned to camouflage the loss of eyelashes by 'dotting' my eyelids with some eyeliner. It was disconcerting how expressionless I looked without any hair to accent my eyes or frame my face. I was determined that, despite this damned disease, I was going to be warm *and* fashionable!

In the beginning, I was an emotional mess. I remember being very tearful when my initial chemotherapy treatment started. The nurse called me to go to the area where they access and flush your port to prepare it for the infusion and to draw the blood lab work. She didn't realize it was my first chemo visit, and she went directly to the infusion area. I was not able to walk as fast as she did and lost her when she turned a corner. I stood in the hallway feeling like a small child lost in the department store and needing my mother. I found her eventually in a work area with curtained spaces.

She was at the far end. I was relieved to find her, but my emotions were overflowing by then, and my eyes were welling with tears. I had just been told moments ago by my Oncologist that my cancer had already spread to my bones, so I was on overload. She noticed I wasn't quite together and leaned in to say very gently, "Is this your first chemo treatment?" With that I had a total meltdown and couldn't stop sobbing.

My Oncologist told me that the recent Pet Scan confirmed my cancer had spread to my bones. Cancerous lesions were found in my left scapula, sternum, thoracic and lumbar spine, sacrum, pelvis and the head of the right femur. The spread seemed so odd to me. I had this instant vision of a bolt of cancer-carrying lightning entering my left shoulder blade and traveling obliquely down my spine and pelvis, then out through my right groin area. That I could understand. But telling me this cancer spread to these areas randomly just seemed so absurd to me. Well, that's cancer for you. OR was it that I was in denial? To me, it seemed this cancer was irrational, and in fact, pretty random.

She asked me if I had experienced any recent pain in my bones or joints. I said that in the past two months, I noticed a sharp pain in my right groin whenever I stepped out of the car on the passenger side. I attributed that to a muscle pull . . . I certainly didn't think as I stepped out of the car, "Oh, I must have cancer in my bones." That never would have dawned on me. The other areas where it was found all happened to be places where I had previously experienced an injury or had a fall. Like the bursitis and torn rotator cuff I've had a number of years in my left shoulder that causes burning pain in the same area where cancerous lesions were found. So I questioned the scan report and thought these could be areas of inflammation and not osseous lesions. PET Scans, while incredibly reliable, are also sensitive tests. I rationalized that the tests were wrong. Being the great Oncologist she is and not wanting to have any area of doubt regarding this life-altering diagnosis, Dr. Ronjon ordered an MRI of the spine and pelvis. It confirmed that osseous lesions were seen that are directly attributed to metastatic cancer in these bones. Now I knew without question and no longer refuted the findings. Acceptance. That's a tough one.

Two weeks prior to that, I met my all female oncology team who were gathered around me in the examining room and palpating the two lesions found, one in each breast. After the exam, each explained their specialty and what they would do for me. I thought I had a curable form of breast cancer at the time. My team consisted of a Radiologist who would prescribe the exact amount of radiation I would need for the large lobular carcinoma in my left breast and the small ductal carcinoma in my right breast. Next, I met the Breast Cancer Specialist who would do the surgery, a mastectomy, following the radiation. A plastic surgeon would be added to the mix later on for the breast reconstruction phase.

Then I met the Oncologist who would follow me medically and prescribe the chemotherapy. And finally, a Nurse Navigator who, I presume, would keep us all from bumping into one another. It felt like I was a beauty queen who was primping and getting glamorized by her personal assistants for the big moment in the spotlight. I know that sounds strange, but they did create an aura of pleasant concern and gentleness. I felt relieved to have these awesome pros all around me. So, now we're a team . . . Rah!! Rah!!

Two weeks later, I dropped my invisible 'Pom Poms' right to the floor. All these great physicians, except my Oncologist, dropped out of the picture as soon as the Staging was done and I was told I had Stage 4 bilateral breast cancer with bone mets! How can that be? A negative mammogram four months before this diagnosis and a negative breast biopsy one year before in the exact same place where I found this mass while showering? I only found it because it was an itchy sensation in my left breast. I thought it was a reaction to something, not cancer.

In fact, I recalled that the stereotactic needle biopsy was performed in that location. And, I recalled my history of reactions to metals, like inert skin staples and pierced earrings. I immediately thought I must have developed adhesions due to a reaction to the needle, and they're making me itchy. But now, I had the feeling that I was going to be headed right for the 'dead letter' office. We were now a team of one, not as much fun. But, in time, we became a formidable team. My awesome Oncologist said she was going to start me on an 'aggressive treatment of chemo drugs. I never once objected. I thought, "Great! She has my back and we are in this together. I'm not going to be sent to the 'dead letter' office!" Seven months later, my PET Scan showed I was in remission. Two years later I am still stable. Woot! Woot!

But I wasn't completely out of the woods. I still had a lot of emotional baggage to deal with. As I already mentioned, I broke down in tears in the Port Access area on day one of chemotherapy. It happened again on the occasion of my second chemo visit. One of the nurses who observed this told me that patients who get a rein on their feelings tend to do better. I looked at her quizzically. She explained that from their experience, there seems to be a link between accepting your diagnosis, getting a handle on your emotions, and having success with treatment. To this day, I don't know if she said that strictly to help me 'buck up' or if her statement is the absolute truth. I don't even want to know. After that visit, I focused on getting my emotions in check. I wasn't going to break down before every treatment. I didn't want to be a casualty. I wanted to succeed. I wanted to live.

So, as I learned, the most important thing is to snap out if it! You can't manage your illness if you don't get back to the real world. You will need the help and support of a number of people. You have to let them in. You can't let anyone in if you're paralyzed by fear. Step away from the door, open it and let them in. I called a 1-800 number provided by an organization called, *Walk in My Shoes*. They put you in touch with a woman who has your exact diagnosis within the next 24 hours. We talked for an hour. But it was her first words that got my attention and gave me a tremendous sense of relief: "Hi Carol, my name is Laurie. I was diagnosed nine years ago with Breast Cancer that metastasized to my bones." Whew, I thought . . . she is still alive nine years later. Could that be me? I hope so." There is nothing like talking to a cancer patient who has been there and knows what you're going through.

Two months after my diagnosis, I told my youngest daughter that the highs and lows of my illness had been pretty extreme so far. I felt like I had climbed into a fragile little toy-like airplane that took off, zoomed around, then dipped into every valley and climbed up every steep mountain while I alternately clenched and unclenched my fingers into tight fists of joy, sadness, anger, despair and shrill laughter arising more out of fear than happiness. I guess its not unusual to have labile feelings like that at this stage. It was exactly 57 days since I learned about these tumors in my breasts. I just wanted them out of my body! It felt so strange and alien at the time.

After learning I was Stage 4, I also discovered I was not a candidate for surgery, i.e., no mastectomy would be performed. My Oncologist explained that with metastasis, you have to focus on managing the metastasis so it doesn't spread more, and not worry about the tumors. The chemo would address them. I guess its only natural to want to be rid of your cancerous tumor. So at first, I felt disappointed.

It was difficult to hear that we were shifting to Plan B . . . this was no longer an A game. I had to accept that whatever was growing in my body was a part of me now . . . we were in this together. I realized you can't really turn on your body, even if it has turned on you. However, this feeling was short-lived. After my chemotherapy, my lobular tumor shrunk 50% and my ductal tumor was gone! As soon as I was in remission and the 'mets' was stable, my Oncologist arranged for me to have a Lumpectomy. I met again with the Breast Cancer Specialist who agreed we would get rid of the primary tumor that was now 50% smaller. Psychologically, it felt great to be rid of it. It's also precautionary surgery, done just in case the cancer comes back.

If it becomes active again, the primary tumor that's sitting in the left breast, could shed cancer cells that could get into the bloodstream or lymph fluid and then travel throughout the body. They could settle in an organ, and if the environment is right for it, begin to duplicate and form a new metastasis. In the case of breast cancer, that's likely to be the lungs, the liver or the brain. I also learned that microscopic cancer cells are circulating throughout your body until you've had successful chemotherapy. Then, they're pretty much gone. Monthly blood work is done to monitor for them. They count how many are seen in a specific volume of blood.

I look for these results every month as proof that I don't have any active disease going on and that I remain in remission. These numeric results are what many call 'tumor markers'. They can cause a lot of anxiety. Add to that the PET scans every six months or so, which are also anxiety-producing, it becomes a way of life for a person with metastasis . . . . it's worse than the lottery!! You can become obsessed with this stuff. It's best not to do it. Some women have told me their tumor markers were way up, but it didn't end up that their cancer was back. Most Oncologists go by how you're feeling and other indicators, not just the numbers. However, it's the nature of the beast that some cancer patients get fixated on their tests and on numbers. I did that initially, but I no longer do . . . . I'm too busy living my life.

I will describe for you in more detail the five phases I experienced as I went through my early stages of diagnosis. It took close to a year for me to feel as I do now, in charge and enjoying each day. I wrote poems throughout each phase and share them with you now. For me, they were very therapeutic and helped me to heal.

Phase 1
Shock and Awe

This is the black hole. It's overwhelming. It's *the 'Knock Me Off My Feet'* feeling that I experienced at the time of my diagnosis. It lasted about two months . . . seriously. It started with a wordless moment in which I thought I 'imagined' what the physician just said to me. Then my hearing and vision seemed temporarily suspended. I felt that my feet were dangling in mid-air and I was going to be sucked into a huge hole. I needed to break this suspended feeling and find a way to say something, anything.

The room had darkened considerably around the edges, but there was a very bright light in the center, although it seemed a distance away. I willed it back into view. I looked at my husband who was standing in the corner with his back to us sniffling quietly, and my youngest daughter who was sitting on the chair weeping softly into a tissue. I was sitting on the edge of the treatment table like I was frozen in time. I finally said, "Well, it could be worse." My Oncologist said nothing. I sensed that she wanted us to have the time to respond or to take it all in before going on. No one said anything. The seconds seemed like hours. After a moment, I said, "Of course, it could be a lot better." The room filled with light, scattered laughs. *Gallows laughter*. It's nervous energy occurring in the form of laughter and released spontaneously after shocking, really bad, 'down on your knees' news. Then it grew solemn again. I said with a calm and reassuring voice for the benefit of my family, "But it could have been worse."

I didn't climb out of this hole until I got on an anti-depressant to balance my mood. I would cry anytime I had to say the words *'I have metastatic breast cancer'*. I can tell you, I haven't cried about my cancer since. Once you get 'out of the hole', you see the light of day and you see everything else clearly. You want to stay on top and in control. You can accomplish more. You could spend energy on getting your 'affairs in order'. That's not a bad idea. But after you've drawn up or reviewed your Living Will, your Last Will and Testament, and have all your financial papers updated and in order, then you should spend time throwing out things you don't want or need. It's a good thing to do no matter what's going on with your health or in your life. After that, plan a trip to a faraway, exotic place you've never seen, plant some flowers, call a friend, or engage your spouse or other significant person in your life to go to a movie or out for dinner. Don't look back. Keep your chin up and your head forward.

"I shall tell you a great secret, my friend. Do not wait for the last judgment. It takes place every day."

Albert Camus, writer and philosopher, 1913-60, from 'La Chute', meaning 'The Fall', 1956.

Lost in a Chemo Haze

I'm lost in a chemo haze beneath a cloud of cancer.
It envelops me and I can't be freed.
I could cry and stomp, scream and shout.
But it's no use . . . I can't get out.

Cancer invades my smallest cells, it's part of me.
It goes where I go, it does what I do.
I can raise my fists in fury or turn away.
But it's futile now, it's destined to stay.

It spreads its powerful wings, from breast to bone.
But quietly encloses over me when I cry alone.
It sends out pain signals from stem to stern.
There's no escape . . . nowhere to turn.

The chemo drugs are like depth charges.
Round 1, Round 2, Round 3, Round 4.
'Look out below! Fire in the hole!'
It shakes me to my very soul.

Scans and labs, MRI's and biopsies,
They look at you from top to bottom.
And then check you inside out,
I'm left with less hope, more doubt.

The misleading false negative tests,
And worthless mammograms.
Breast density that shrouds the lesion,
Allowed to grow beyond all reason.

There's no reach to recovery,
No pink ribbon cure.
The goal now is remission,
But isn't that just a 'stay of execution'?

Where were all those curious minds?
And why didn't they stop the spread,
. . . when this was just a seed?
I know back then I could have been freed.

The Monster in the Closet

There's a monster in my closet,
A huge spider on the wall,
Green snakes under my bed.
Mice scampering down the hall.

Scary words and alarming pictures,
Are forever etched inside my brain.
They conjure up deathly images,
Haunting me over and over again.

No one wants to bring it up,
It's the elephant in the room.
So we talk of news and weather,
No one needs gloom and doom.

No other malady makes us cringe,
Here's why I think it's so.
Cancer carries with it a stigma,
It's like a fatal blow.

And it forces us to face,
Our grim mortality.
Society shies away from this,
It values youthful vitality.

So a subculture has sprung up,
To support emotions and psyche.
Online groups full of camaraderie,
Free massage therapy and Reiki.

Ultra modern cancer centers,
Research labs work diligently,
Science pushes treatment further,
Pink fundraisers work tirelessly.

Helpful social services abound,
Spiritual supports for the soul.
Hospice services to cradle you,
When cancer finally takes its toll.

But something's wrong with this picture,
Despite these services and much more.
All around I see my suffering sisters,
'Won't someone cure us?' I implore.

I Feel it in My Bones

I can feel it in my bones,
Pain like I slept on stones.
I feel the usual dread,
A damp, rainy day lies ahead.

Like a creaky ship run aground,
I barely make my way around.
I've gotten used to the pain,
Not the ebbing energy drain.

Then came MRI's and Scans,
To change my future plans.
New problem in the bone,
Worse than I could've known.

Its not about getting old,
There's a new story to be told.
The breast cancer has spread,
Into the right femoral head.

Down through pelvis and sternum,
Into the lower spine and sacrum.
Oddly, cancer cells now hide,
In the shoulder blade on my left side.

Eaten away bone seems like treason,
As it leads to weakened bony lesions.
It eventually turns to Swiss cheese,
Attacking the chest down to the knees.

It spares the lower legs and arms.
Neither the toes nor fingers it harms.
Still there is pain in these parts,
Arthritis stings like pointed darts.

What made this cancer grow?
And how could I not know?
What a mystery is this disease,
Baffling scholars for centuries.

Will they ever discover a cure?
They can't seem to say for sure.
Guess I'll just ask for prayers,
Or get more empty stares.

They have raised more than a billion.
To stem the tide of this nasty villain.
But no one has found a lasting cure,
It won't be found in races that's for sure!

"It's not enough to have lived. We should be determined to live for something. May I suggest that it be creating joy for others, sharing what we have for the betterment of person kind, bringing hope to the lost and love to the lonely."

—Leo F Buscaglia

Broken

I'M BROKEN . . .

Like the clock in the hall,
It stands so straight and tall,
But chimes twice when it's one,
Inside the damage has been done.
No matter that its an heirloom,
Its headed for the trash room.

I'M BROKEN . . .

Like my childhood china doll,
The victim of an errant ball.
Once wore a wide-brimmed hat,
Head shattered by a youthful bat.
She lies discarded in a heap,
Destined for a hole six feet deep.

I'M BROKEN . . .

No longer strong in the saddle,
I've been thrust into a battle.
My invisible scars are all inside,
Flesh weak, spirit lost its pride.
Cancer runs pretty deep,
Can't shake it off even when asleep.

I'M BROKEN . . .

Incurable illness is a game-changer,
My life keeps getting stranger.
I wake at night in a cold sweat,
To whom do I owe this debt?
I feel so horribly off-track,
Desperately want to send it back!

I'M BROKEN . . .

No more wishing and hoping,
I'm just adjusting and coping.
Perhaps I could fill in every crack,
Unlike my doll in the discard sack.
Fix the clock to chime again,
Live in a peaceful state of Zen.

Phase 2
Betrayal and Despair

Learning that I had Stage 4 Breast Cancer with my first cancer diagnosis went beyond shocking . . . I felt betrayed by the medical community. Faithfully getting annual mammograms that proved negative, with the exception of one the previous year . . . but that was followed up by a stereotactic breast biopsy that came back negative . . . I clearly felt let down, in fact . . . it was more like I fell between the cracks and into a hole that went to the deepest caverns of the earth's core . . . too far to be reached. So, the tumor grew and grew. It had no choice. It gave out its typical warnings, but they weren't heeded.

How is it possible that with the annual screenings, it was *my* find?? Did I ever in my wildest dreams think that I would find this while showering. Millions of women do self breast exams all the time, but I expect they pray that they don't find a curious lump or thickening . . . they pray, "Please Dear God, let me get through this quickly and get on with my life. Let me not find ANYTHING that's suspicious . . . . please Dear God, please." Or maybe they just hold their breath . . . but I bet that none are thinking they're going to come up with a Stage 4 tumor that's harder than rock, a long and spiraling mass that seems to tunnel inward to the center of the breast, until you can't reach the end of it . . . neither did I. But, that's my story.

"Carol, this has been growing for a long, long time." my Oncologist said. She said it was a slow growing tumor . . . I suppose that's the one comfort I have. It grew slowly. No one knew.

"Carol, when we look at your mammograms, all we see are white clouds. You have very dense breast tissue. We couldn't see the tumor lurking in there."

I met with the Breast Cancer Specialist who was going to perform my Lumpectomy. When I asked her why follow-up tests aren't done on women with dense breast tissue, she said "Insurance won't pay for it". I asked why? I thought this might have made a difference in my case. My tumor could have been found at Stage 1 or 2; hell, I'd even be happy with Stage 3. But jumping into the game at Stage 4 is a lousy place to start.

She said they won't pay because there are too many 'false positives'. Trying to take this in, I couldn't help but wonder, "How many is too many?" If, for example, they do 100 follow-ups on women with dense breast tissue and only two women are found to have a tumor in the breast tissue, "Are these two lives not worth the cost of those 98 who turn out to be false positives?" What is the threshold? In a similar situation, the Federal Drug Administration announced their recommendation to take a specific drug off the market for breast cancer treatment that had been in use for at least a year.

Clinical trials showed this drug ONLY helped 50% of the women who were given the drug infusion. Why isn't that good enough? They also claimed it had potential side effects that were too serious to warrant keeping it on the market. They cited the possibility of severe bleeding. Well, I don't think there is a chemo agent without potential for serious side effects, like kidney damage, for example. However, the drug was going to continue to be given to people with other types of cancer, like colon cancer, for example. So, why aren't they worried they might hemorrhage or bleed out? Why should breast cancer patients be left out?

Consider that this relatively new drug is somewhat expensive as compared to the traditional cytotoxic agents. It serves to deplete the tumor of all its blood supply, hoping it will dry up and go away. Looking at this objectively, I ask myself, "So are they taking this away from breast cancer patients, many whose lives have been saved by this drug, because there are too many of us to be treated?" If I follow that line of thinking, I'm led to believe that womankind has been hung out to dry. It's just too expensive to keep us alive. So they'll go on to save the other folks who don't have breast cancer. Sorry, I feel that's how it stacks up. Its about the money. it's the "Do the best for the most with the least amount of money" philosophy put into play.

I was on this drug during my second treatment regimen. It was coupled with a typical cytotoxic agent. However, after the fourth dose, my platelet count was progressively dropping and my oncologist was concerned. While I didn't have any active bleeding, I had some bleeding if I blew my nose, bruised easily and noticed my fingernails getting a light purple. I became vigilant and watched my gums, stools and urine for any signs of bleeding. I never experienced any active bleeding after having four rounds of the drug, but my platelet count never came back up quite enough to warrant taking the risk.

Two years later, my platelet count has finally come back where it belongs. I was never put back on the controversial drug. This occurred during the height of the admonitions from the FDA and hearings being held with the drug manufacturer and pharmaceutical company. Some women were testifying at hearings that their lives had been extended due to the efficacy of this drug and were pleading with the FDA to keep it on the market. There were also children of some of these moms who were in the center of the fray, writing letters and being interviewed for newspaper stories.

It was quite upsetting and most likely very effective to see a photo in the news of a teenager begging the government to keep his mother alive and to let her continue getting this drug. In my case, fortunately, my Oncologist and I felt things were going well enough without this drug at the time. I didn't concern myself any more other than noting what was going on nationally. Although, it does seem to have died down, I imagine it can be ordered by a physician if he or she makes a good case for it.

Metastatic Madness

You have to be half-mad,
To live with this disease.
It seems to have a way,
Of bringing you to your knees.

Cancer cells invade your body,
And soon they settle in.
Uninvited and unwanted,
The beast beneath your skin.

The big bad chemo drugs, like a tsunami,
Blew it all away.
But like the worst kind of nightmare,
It will return someday.

You don't know when, you don't know how,
You only know it will.
So you clean closets, throw out old papers,
And update your Living Will.

People say, "We're all going to die,
. . . each one of us.
Tomorrow, I could go out,
And get hit by a car or bus."

If I stepped off a curb,
And got mowed down by a truck.
How quick an end that would be,
Not this agonizing one, just my luck.

Treatment means constant oversight,
By my oncologist and her team.
I accept that I must comply,
But inside I want to scream.

And all the while I pray,
It won't ruin my life plan.
I'd like to see my grandson,
Grow up to be a man.

And see my friends and family,
For just a little longer.
Doesn't seem like much to ask,
From the 'evil cancer monger'.

Tumor markers, cancer antigens,
Scans and other tests.
Rule my world like the cancer,
In my bones and both my breasts.

The truly maddening part is that,
One day it will spread too far.
How will I cope as I begin to fade,
Just like a falling star?

No one knows what lies ahead,
As we don't have a crystal ball,
All we know is we want someone,
To catch us when we fall.

*"Courage is not the towering oak that sees storms
come and go; it is the fragile blossom that opens
in the snow."*

Alice Mackenzie Swaim

Scanxiety

Do you fear you've lost all belief?
Worry chemo won't provide relief?

Are you worried there is no hope?
And you fear you just can't cope?

You are not alone, for so many wait,
Like you, they obsess over their fate.

But cancer is truly a waiting game,
It's like staring at the Eternal Flame.

'Scanxiety' is such a dreaded feeling,
It consumes you till your mind is reeling.

You'll need great patience waiting for your tests,
You'll worry and fret more, while eating less.

Even waiting for a routine scan result,
Can turn out to be the most difficult.

Each time, your life hangs in the balance,
No one can correct your feeling of imbalance.

You will need several books on the shelf,
Be sure you avoid waiting by yourself.

You might work on puzzles while you lurk,
Always worrying, 'Did my treatment work?'

Ask someone to sit with you by the phone,
Good news or bad, no one should be alone.

You think you'll conquer this obsession,
You pray to hear 'There's no progression'.

Party In Cancerville

It's party time in Cancerville,
It comes this time each year.
Leaves of Fall turn green to red,
And Octoberfests appear.

With a flurry of pink ribbons,
Ads promote products in cheery pink.
They make me feel sad inside,
And my spirits start to sink.

Relay races and fundraisers,
Hail our long-suffering disease.
They treat us just like heroes,
To make us feel at ease.

But I don't feel easy,
In fact, it worries me a lot.
The stench of corporate business,
My cancer and I can't be bought.

We don't wish to sell out to them,
They profit despite our objection.
Earning bundles from misfortune,
Huge salaries for the corporation.

It seems to me the wrong approach,
To make light of a serious condition.
Ignoring those of us with metastasis,
They seem to act without contrition.

Ignoring all the projections,
Of a high recurrence ratio.
There are thirty in a hundred,
Who will recur in a year or so.

But the fun goes on in Cancerville,
They simply shake off our dread.
They celebrate sainted survivors,
Who perhaps soon will be dead.

Plied with talk of cures,
And of being cancer free.
Those with early stage cancer,
Aren't told how fatal it can be.

Friendships that Hold
& Those that Grow Cold

Some friends come and some friends go,
Some feel they've had enough and just blow.
They might say they'll call you soon enough,
But that won't happen, you find it's all a bluff.

You check email daily, then you feel rejected.
Facebook disappoints, blocked as you expected.
Some friends are scared, and likely to unhinge,
They imagine deathbed scenes that make them cringe.

My life isn't just about dying, so little do they know,
I'm geared more to living and being on the go.
Some friends take you away from the daily grind,
They distract you to keep you in a good frame of mind.

Those are the golden ones, caring, selfless and kind,
Those who abandon you are in some ways blind.
Don't give it another thought as they slip out the door,
For shallow friends possess traits that you deplore.

What goes around comes around, as some people say,
So-called friends will face their own mortality some day.
By then it may be too late to patch up what you had,
A friendship shattered in a million pieces is quite sad.

You can't hold on to those who run when you are in need,
Their day will come to face those flaws, a hard lesson indeed.
True friendship will always be there, through thick or thin,
Life is much too precious to waste on fair-weather kin.

Phase 3
Loneliness & Loathing

Cancer can cause you to feel lonely even when you're not alone. Unless you're in a room with people who have cancer, you can't help but feel different. This feeling that sets you apart, puts some distance between you and others. You don't will it and they may not even be aware of it, but it's there. I often found myself immersed in wild thoughts careening through my day, of a shortened life, losing all that I hold dear, not being able to see things through that matter to me, not seeing young family members achieve their various milestones in life, or even see my young grandson of three enter kindergarten. No one will live forever, but this terminal existence is like a time bomb ticking inside your head. It can consume you. It's unnerving. Its not just life changing, its life ending.

Loathing this disease came very easily to me. Cancer conjures up images of disease riddled bodies wracked with pain, emaciated, weakened and numbed by narcotics, gasping for every breathe while praying to die. What other beast does this to the human body and mind over a prolonged period of time? Every aspect of it is ugly, mean and cold. And there are so many forms of cancer, afflicting so many organs and body parts. Worst of all, it kills children and makes them suffer horribly. How bad is that? It doesn't get much worse than killing young children. That gives me nightmares.

No one is immune to it. Prevention may help somewhat, but there are no guarantees for avoiding this aggressive illness. You can be a non-smoker who eats healthy and exercises, doesn't drink, avoids sun exposure and pollutants . . . and still be taken down by cancer. It invades the bodies of every race and gender, all ethnicities and age groups, the rich and the poor, illiterate and college educated, ignorant and caring. Even animals aren't immune from this indiscriminate invader. It imbeds itself into the skin, can reside in nearly every organ, eats away at bone; permeates soft tissue, hard tissue and body fluids . . . it's a master destroyer and plunderer of families, stable homes, good memories and all things worth treasuring. Once it resides inside you, its eager to take over if left untreated. It multiplies, divides, spreads, triangulates, gets into the lymph fluid, flows through the bloodstream, and eventually is found in most all body fluids where it infests. Microscopic cancer cells that can't even be detected float around looking to make a 'nest' somewhere . . . anywhere it finds amenable to its needs . . . a blood supply being chief among them. It's an insatiable, life-sucking monster.

Life in the Chemo Lane

Life in the chemo lane,
Doesn't go 100 miles per hour.
It's more like 10 or 15 MPH,
All uphill and losing power.

You wait, then wait some more,
It becomes the rule of thumb.
You wait on treatment days,
Until you're feeling numb.

Life in the chemo lane means you,
Constantly brace yourself for the call.
You know, the one in which,
You're waiting for the 'other foot' to fall.

It could be your last MRI,
Recent CT or PET Scan.
You tell yourself over & over,
'I can do this, I know I can.'

Life in the chemo lane,
Doesn't promise to be fun.
Unless you like wearing a wig,
Out in the blazing sun.

Changes occur as hair thins and falls out,
Even eyebrows and eyelashes fade.
Nails sport a funky purple color,
Your nose runs and you feel betrayed.

Life in the chemo lane,
Is no trip to the beach or the ocean.
It's endless injections and infusions,
As researchers seek a magic potion.

It's reading & plowing through,
Every cancer article you can find.
It's an insatiable thirst for knowledge,
You keep stuffing it in your mind.

Life in the chemo lane,
May not be your thing.
If you fear sharp needles,
Or freak out from their sting.

You may lose your appetite,
A sense of taste or smell you lack.
It may be more than you can handle,
As you beg for your old life back.

Life in the chemo lane,
Simply put isn't all that great.
But for now it's all I've got,
And it controls my fate.

Like a junkie who needs a fix,
I seek toxic drugs for a big cell kill.
Load me up, forget the side effects,
And don't worry about the bill.

Life in the chemo lane,
Will eventually come to an end.
And if these drugs do their job,
I'll be glad to call them 'friend'.

I know that sounds crazy,
But what doesn't kill you makes you strong.
Until science makes a breakthrough,
My oncologist can do no wrong.

My Grandfather's Sleeping

My grandfather's sleeping
Yet he murmurs a sound.
It's a low and hushed warning,
That falls to the ground.

I lean in much closer,
To hear the next sound he utters,
But he lies still now,
He no longer mutters.

His hand has now fallen,
Away from his side,
I can't bear to look,
My Grandfather has died.

*"Do not go gentle into that good night, old age should
Burn and rave at close of day; Rage, rage against the
dying of the light."*

Dylan Thomas

She Lies There Sleeping

She lies there sleeping,
I sit here weeping.
Weeping for how things used to be,
Waiting for her to slip away quietly.

I thought I'd be the strong one at the end,
But she's much stronger, my lover, my friend.
How long has it been since cancer made its arrival?
We stopped counting and focused on her survival.

But who could forget the day or even the hour,
That she quietly approached me after her shower?
She said she had an area that was itchy 'inside',
She found this hard lumpy mass on her left side.

In a trembling voice she said something's very wrong,
The thickening she found was at least two inches long.
Her dense breasts blocked the tumors from their vision,
White shadows on 'mammos' caused much indecision.

Those false negative results were like a bad rumor,
There's suspicion but no proof of the growing tumor.
The biopsy needle never found the target,
We learned to forgive, but won't ever forget.

After that day, our lives went out of control,
We didn't know it would take such a heavy toll.
She endured so many tests that wore her out,
Producing results that left us with little doubt.

So now after all the chemo, surgery, and praying,
We've come to know that only her memory's staying.
She will be joining all the other angels above,
As her suffering could not be cured by our love.

He Sits There Weeping

He sits there weeping,
While I lay sleeping.
He weeps for how things used to be,
He thinks I'm asleep, but I can see.

I thought he'd be the stronger one in the end,
He struggles to get through it, my lover, my friend.
I remember how it all began, both the day and the hour,
That strange breast thickening that I found in the shower.

My breast was just itchy, I thought it was scar tissue,
I had a negative breast biopsy, it didn't seem an issue.
But something was wrong, it was too big, too hard a mass,
It was one of those moments you wish would just pass.

But there's no way to easily climb out of this hole,
You call for help while you pray for your soul.
Seven years later, we can no longer hold it at bay,
Its time to light candles, and once again we pray.

Cancer is a wily beast, it lives, it spreads, it breathes,
It destroys all in its path, and it mutates as it seethes.
It will find one in three who will eventually be harmed,
Like a wild epidemic, why isn't everyone alarmed!?

It takes you whether your child is young or your parents are old,
Not discriminating, it takes the poor and those with piles of gold.
It takes your hair, strips away your pride, disrupts your memory,
It will lower your blood cells draining you of all your energy.

It doesn't ever feel your pain or bow to anyone's sympathy,
But it can't take away your love of family or your integrity.
It's time for me to go, the angels spread their wings over me,
I depart this world of suffering and leave just a memory.

Undying Love

Soft brown eyes follow me every waking hour,
The only time we part is when I'm in the shower.
Our 'rescue' dog came with deep unabated fears,
She had been traumatized in her few short years.

She runs off hurriedly when any water is run,
Abandoned and abused, the damage is done.
She was intended to be my husband's pet,
But bonded with me the moment we met.

We worked with her to lessen the panic,
Over time, responses were less frantic.
Feral when found and begging for food,
Seeking sustenance wherever she could.

Florist shop employees recognized the signs,
She was homeless, no need to read minds.
This little runaway needed help and a home,
Their assistance would end her need to roam.

Delighted with being fed, and pretty grateful too,
They named her 'Flora' then decided what to do.
They called a pet sanctuary for adoption help,
"Want a new home ?" she gave a giant 'Yelp'.

Flora was at the *Waggin' Tails Pet Adoption Day*,
She picked us right out and stole our hearts away.
We brought our family to get the group reaction,
She seemed a good fit and gave us all affection.

Choosing a dog is an important decision,
Your home and lifestyle will need revision.
But arriving home, she bolted out of the car,
Frightened and confused, she ran quite far.

We searched that whole day and into the night,
No amount of praying could make this right.
We called the *Waggin' Tails* folks who soon came by,
They weren't nearly as worried as my husband and I.

Familiar voices and whistles quickly coaxed her out,
'Will she ever adjust to us?' I asked with some doubt.
But now we are bonded tightly as two could be,
Always nearby, she gives her undying love to me.

Being a canine, she knew of my cancer before me,
Likely sensing the change in my body's chemistry.
She nuzzles nearby, I feel each puff of warm breath,
Sniffing and licking me, she worries about my death.

Its known that dogs smell cancer and respond in kind,
As we lay, I pet her silky coat and her gaze meets mine.
We stay that way for hours, not worrying what's in store,
Her wet black nose nudges me to pet her more.

I never would have expected loyalty to this degree,
This loving creature makes no move without me.
Even when hospitalized briefly last year,
She kept a vigil, waiting for me to reappear.

When I returned, she jumped right into the air,
Her pure joy was almost more than I could bear.
She's very protective now, knowing I'm not well,
Always at my side and ready to give intruders hell.

Through months of chemo, she lay next to me,
No matter when I arise, she's the best company.
Flora is a companion who helps me through each day,
And expects very little for the love she gives away.
I can't imagine life without my loyal friend,
Her warmth will comfort me to the very end.

Phase 4
Complying & Compensating

As a cancer patient, you soon discover that to have any hope of a decent quality of life, you need to cooperate with the treatment plan and, more importantly, you need to become a part of the oncology team. The latter means speaking up, participating, and making your needs and preferences known. This involves learning something about your diagnosis and available options. There is more than you can shake a stick at online. But, be sure you go only to valid and recognized websites, like the American Cancer Society, National Cancer Institute and the Centers for Disease Control and Prevention. For metastatic breast cancer patients, there is METAvivor, the Metastatic Breast Cancer Network and Advanced Breast Cancer for starters.

I also joined an online group at www.bcmets.org that is just loaded with resources and information from a few experts in the field of metastatic breast cancer treatment and an up-to-date, knowledgeable and sharing group of men and women, all who have metastatic breast cancer. They advocate for themselves and each other just by keeping up with the information posted there daily. It can be anything, from new drugs, to clinical trials, to funding for research, new treatments in the pipeline, managing side effects, coping with your illness day to day, dealing with family, tips for managing diarrhea, pain, dry skin, nutrition, fatigue, etc. This group keeps up with one another, sometimes meeting up at conferences and conventions, and occasionally in private email chats to discuss more sensitive issues that need one-on-one follow-up. They grieve when a member dies, they cheer when someone has success with their treatment to curtail progression or recurrence of their cancer, and finally achieve a state of remission or no evidence of disease, encourage them when it seems like they can't go on due to problems with their chemotherapy, hormonal treatments or radiation, and wish them well when surgery is around the corner. They become family.

After awhile, you realize you have become a member of this family too and feel good about rooting with them. You wouldn't feel this way if you hadn't at some point after diagnosis begun to compensate for what cancer has taken away from you. It may have robbed you of a lot of your energy and feeling of well-being, but you have made up for that in the level of interest you have taken in learning about your disease and conquering some of what it has to dish out. You may not be cured and you may not live a whole lot longer than the predicted lifespan you have been advised of, but you will do everything within your capability to overcome side effects, preserve your life and keep your spirits up . . . . at least, that's what I did. An antidepressant picked my mood right up. After that, I felt indomitable. I believed I could take on this bully that had come into my life and show it a thing or two. Come on cancer, I'm ready for you!

The Winter of My Chemo Tent

It's the dead of winter,
I feel it deep within my bones,
I hunker down as howling winds,
Race madly over frozen ground.

A flurry of snowflakes dance upward,
Then sideways and around,
They fall gently, gently, gently,
A white blanket lands with no sound.

I sit here waiting for,
Another round of chemo to pass.
To utter the words 'I have cancer'
Still makes my heart pound.

My world is rocked by my diagnosis,
And all the weird and grueling tests.
Shocked by these Stage IV tumors,
Growing in both my breasts.

❧❧❧❧❧

Since this life-changing illness started
And these breast tumors were found,
It's been really hard to find cover
And put my tent into the ground.

I need my tent to protect me,
From all this toxic stuff,
That's seeping through my veins,
Making my life unbearably rough.

I know it's a necessary evil,
And I pray it does its thing.
Just need to know I've got my tent up,
To soften the blow and blunt the sting.

My tent is white and it's very strong,
Made to withstand a severe winter blizzard.
With tentacles that can go clear through to China,
All I really need now is a 'pup tent wizard'.

❧❧❧❧

But what is that in the distance I see?
In a long flowing cape that flutters to and fro.
Maybe it's the 'wizard' coming to help,
I squint to see clearly through the swirling snow.

As the figure comes nearer, it oddly reveals,
A softly rounded woman heading towards me.
She tightens her hood and smoothes her furled cape,
Then openly announces, 'I've come to set you free!'

Oh no, I plead, I'm so not ready for that!
Do not fear, she says, this isn't nearly the end.
She leans in against the wind to whisper in my ear,
I'm here about your tent my dear new friend.

I know that you've been feeling quite low,
With your chemo tent still lying in the snow.
It seems you've been struggling so very hard,
Against a simple truth you seem not to know.

Your greatest strength comes from deep inside,
You need no tent to shield you from the toxic storm.
Truly believing in yourself will see you through,
Its all you need to stay safe and warm.

I learned to be strong on that cold winter day,
Now those invasive tumors that spread to my bone,
Don't scare me or make me run for my tent,
With strength and love around me, I'm never alone.

I can focus now on life's great journey,
While I travel from place to place.
Making new friends and meeting with old,
I know now there's no problem I can't face.

Is it Really Me?

Woke up

No hair

Energy gone

Skin so pale

Nails purple

Chemo day

Too tired

Long drive

Infusion longer

Eyelids heavy

Even without lashes

always feel cold

Need someone to hold

Nails keep breaking

I'm always shaking

This isn't me

A new identity

Eyebrows gone

no expression

Is it really me?

If I don't look it?

I guess it is . . .

time to book it!

State of the Art Cancer

I have 'state of the art' cancer,
For every question there's an answer.
Individualized chemotherapy? We got it!
Targeted therapy? No prob . . . we got it!

Want it given through a port?
Or injected in your butt?
We can give your chemo with a pill,
'Oh . . . . my heart be still!'

Want to join an experimental trial?
Our goal is to go the extra mile!
Our Über modern infusion center has it all,
Your own TV, computer, and even a waterfall!

We guarantee our Oncology Team is first rate,
And their knowledge base and 'certs' are up to date.
Our nurses are so compassionate & caring,
They comfort you when treatment's overbearing,

We are a comprehensive cancer center,
Offering 'state of the art' care to all who enter.
Sleek MRI equipment and ultra cool scanners,
We hired the very best architects and planners.

Rapid turnaround time on results of tests,
And our radiation treatment's the very best.
But most of all, we offer care you can afford,
I was so impressed, I jumped onboard!

Wait! Just one more thing, I have a question,
They nod with uncurbed enthusiasm, no hesitation.
When will there be a cure for my cancer?
Oh! Sorry, for that we have no answer.

Remission, Intermission

For those who are in remission,
It's just like an intermission.
The calm before the storm,
A lull before tornado funnels form.

You are free to enjoy your life again,
And forget how really sick you've been.
Even if it doesn't last very long,
The joy and memories will stay strong.

You'll have them with you till the end,
When its time to go 'round the final bend.
Don't be sad or shed many tears,
Put aside the worst of your fears.

Around that bend you're free from fear,
No pain or discomfort you'll found here.
Your spirit will soar in the *Great Beyond*,
You'll rejoin those who have passed on.

You never dreamed of such a special place,
You glide serenely in a cloud-filled space.
You see your earthly loved ones from here,
From this far away heavenly atmosphere.

They're saddened and miss you so for now,
But you know they'll heal again somehow.
You've gracefully accepted this is your fate,
Though you were taken from a loving mate.

You've been told this is the *Great Beyond*,
Where the Angels sing all day long.
It's like nothing you've seen before.
All you know is that you want more.

"Death was a friend, and sleep was Death's brother"

John Steinbeck, *The Grapes of Wrath*

Chemo Brain

Once again, she stood in line,
Swaying slowly to and fro.
Feeling it's all vaguely familiar,
But not sure where to go.

Balding head covered with a wig,
Picked up at a second hand store.
But in her present frame of mind,
A *crown of thorns* would suit her more.

Oblivious to the receding line,
Or worried faces of all who enter.
Her thoughts were interrupted by,
The gatekeeper of the Cancer Center.

'Next!' said the registration clerk,
With that slight lilt in her voice,
'Can I help you?' she chirped,
As though there's another choice.

'Can you help me!?!'
She thought in her head.
No one can help me,
I may as well be dead!

My husband's gone,
No kids to love.
This isn't quite the life,
I had ever dreamed of.

With a quick shuffle of papers,
And an ID Band snapped in place.
She trudged on to the lab's long line,
This time jostling for a space.

Why are they drawing more blood?
My blood counts have been so low.
She was barely among the living,
This cancer had been such a blow.

She'd been so forgetful of late,
But knew this was infusion day.
She bravely braced herself,
Toxic drugs were on their way.

While her oncologist assured her,
Forgetfulness is just another phase.
She still pondered why she can't recall
Anything worthwhile from past days.

Her thoughts once flowed freely,
Just like melted butter.
Now stop, start and loop around,
Then die off without a sputter.

'Can I help you?' once more she hears,
This time it's a steely-eyed lab tech.
'Yes, you can help get my memory back,
For that, I'd write you a big fat check!'

Next came a nurse to greet her,
And then gently guided her in.
The infusion room was humming,
She remembered now where she'd been.

She also remembered the nurse,
Preparing the memory-killing brew.
Three more rounds of that nasty stuff,
And finally she'd be through!

It struck her that her recent days,
Had been filled with too much strife.
The staff challenged her to live longer,
If she would just turn around her life.

'Well maybe I could give it a try,
I need to pray for healing power.
Then I'll give thanks for every day,
Even promise to cherish every hour.'

Could it be just that simple?
Does she still have the will?
You don't know until you try,
Her life was at a standstill.

Somehow she found the strength,
To change how cancer made her feel,
Figuring she'd finally hit bottom,
She quickly got down to kneel.

She found praying wasn't hard,
Her remorse cried to be let out.
Feelings that were dammed up,
And regrets that made her doubt.

Since her recent turnaround,
Chemo day is not so dreary.
She greets everyone she meets,
With a genuine smile that's cheery.

Soon the valet and the lab tech,
And all the registration clerks.
Remember her smiling face,
And give her lots of perks.

She's now one of their favorites,
And every time that she arrives.
They see a renewed woman,
Who's learned how to survive.

They run to get her coffee,
And provide her with a snack.
They say how great she looks,
And always welcome her back.

Her chemo brain is still around,
Taking her old memories away.
But new ones are much better,
So it's really all okay.

She's still a little scared,
Occasionally hesitant and shy.
But she's learned how to live,
And forgotten she will die.

'Thank you dear God,
For showing me the way.
You made it easy for me to see,
A path to brighten my day.'

When the sad day finally came,
And she couldn't hold on anymore.
We heard that this lonely widow,
Had mourners lined up at the door.

Honoring this 'forgetful' woman,
While placing flowers on her grave.
So many came to say goodbye,
To a woman who was so brave.

"Death is nothing else but going home to God,
the bond of love will be unbroken for all eternity."

~ Mother Teresa ~

The Metsters Club

I belong to an exclusive club,
We are known as the 'Metsters'
We don't ride Motorcycles,
And we are not hipsters.

It's for certain people only,
Not everyone would join this club,
We're not discriminating,
And it's not a social snub.

We exist to help each other,
Our members are so caring.
Much knowledge goes around,
And members are always sharing.

We've grown close like sisters,
Although most never meet.
We communicate online daily,
Keeping each other on our feet.

This is a special kind of club
Everyone is dying to join,
We have Metastatic Breast Cancer,
Stage IV is a kick to the groin.

Please don't be mistaken,
Pity is not what we need.
We just want a fair shake,
And also to be freed.

So little funds pour into our cause,
New research is downright dour.
We need someone to champion us,
So many are dying by the hour*.

*Every 13 minutes, a woman in the United States dies from cancer. That's nearly 5 per hour.

Phase 5
Adapting & Advocating

Once you have soldiered on for awhile and learned all you can do to manage your cancer with a specific treatment plan, you begin to look around you and see beyond the tips of your fingers. You are finally stable and feeling more like your old self, except for the lingering fatigue and joint or muscle aches and pains. It may not be time to party yet, but it's certainly time to look around at how you can improve the quality of your life. I may not be around as long as I had hoped, but I soon came to this conclusion:

"If you can't put more years into your life, put more life into your years!"

This is the realization I came to about a year after diagnosis. I had gone through the grueling part of treatment and my Oncologist proudly proclaimed I was in remission. Well, I thought, now what will I do with the rest of my life. It has now been handed back to me and I want to cherish it, like you do when you find a lost and expensive piece of jewelry. You value it more than ever and don't want to lose it again, at least not right away. So, with renewed vigor, you begin to assess where you're at and if you missed anything along the way. You also vow not to miss anything else that comes your way, unless you truly don't have the energy.

I started to reconnect with friends from the past. I got involved with my high school's 50th year class reunion. Despite the fact that I had only gone to one reunion over the past five decades, I had a great desire to become involved. I went to a meeting with an old school chum I had kept in touch with over the years. I found that I really enjoyed seeing a group of my former classmates. They were all so friendly and I felt right at home with them. I dove into the preparations and attended other meetings, finding that the familiarity with people from my past was comforting. I had a great time at the reunion and danced to some of the 'oldies' that I loved as a young girl. It was reinvigorating. I felt more alive than I had for a long time. It was great seeing all those faces from the past . . . they were my past. When your future becomes uncertain, you're past becomes all the more valuable.

Along these same lines, I attended the Annual Tea of my nursing school alma mater. This nursing luncheon is held every year, but I had never participated. Attendees are comprised of alumnae from the early days attending my school of nursing. It was strange to see some of the retired Head Nurses and Supervisors I feared or revered when I was a young 'probie'. It brought back a lot of memories. I also met up with two of my former classmates. They are hospice nurses, one retired and one still working part-time. I felt comfortable enough with them to discuss my diagnosis. We have kept in touch by email since then and I even met one of them for lunch. It's been delightful to reacquaint myself with these people who are part of my history.

Having established a 'circle of support' when I was first diagnosed, gave me a great group of women to keep in touch with on a continuing basis. It wasn't all cancer-related communications. Sometimes, it was just sharing some news and having a laugh or two. One of my former nurse co-workers, Verna Saleski, Coordinator at the Penn State University, Scranton campus, asked me to speak to a group of nursing students about my breast cancer experience. I accepted the invitation and brushed up on my statistics and latest treatment regimens. It was a rewarding day for me as they were an eager group of students. I told them as much as possible to inform them of the latest advances in breast cancer, and help them to develop an inner conscience about doing self-breast exams, religiously! After my experience, I don't think anyone should put all their trust in a single test, that being a mammogram.

My desire to help others now was fueled by my stable condition. I had more energy and was fully recovered from the initial shock and loathing. Psychologically, I think if you are helping others, it's a good sign that you must be doing OK. As simplistic as that sounds, it worked for me. It's good to help others as it comes back to you in so many ways. I think it might help circulate those good 'pheromes' in your body. I no longer felt the need for a support group, but I wanted to help get one off the ground for women with metastatic breast cancer. I felt these women needed their own support sessions and should not be mixed in with women who have early stage breast cancer. Their needs and concerns differ too much to mix them together. Also, those with Stages 1 to 3 might fear being in a group whose prognosis is not as rosy as theirs. The difference is like night and day. The new group met at a cancer wellness center where I had gone for some massage therapy and Reiki.

I don't want to infer that once you have cancer, you are indebted or obligated in some way to help carry the burden of others, or to do charitable works for other cancer patients. I'm just saying that if you are of a mind and body to do so, it will pay off. You'll feel good about yourself and rise above your illness. Lord knows we can use all the help we can get to feel good. I'm not holding my breath waiting for a cure . . . maybe the next generation will have that luxury. For me, its all about pulling myself up by my bootstraps and to keep moving forward. Not that I haven't had a lot of help getting to the point where I am. It's all about what you do with your renewed vigor and strength at this stage.

No Bravery Medal

There's no bravery medal for folks with cancer,
There's no Purple Hearts for Moms who die.
There aren't any taps played at your funeral,
Even if they stand tall when your hearse goes by.

There is talk of a battle that your waging,
And survivor stories surely do abound,
But deep inside you know that you are dying,
A cure it seems is never to be found.

There's no bravery medal for folks with cancer,
Despite being on the front all these lonely days,
Instead of medals you wear your 'chest port' proudly
For the life-extending role that it plays.

Since any chance of getting better still eludes you,
You bow your head when tumor cell counts have risen,
You wait for scans that look inside to tell your story,
Like a fighter in the ring waits for the 'big decision'.

There's no bravery medal for folks with cancer,
Despite the invading enemy you deal with every day,
There's not a jury that would ever find you guilty,
If you consider going AWOL and running far away.

But you can't really run away from yourself,
Or hang up your gloves to leave the boxing ring,
So you soldier on and stop your lips from trembling,
Then wipe the tear from your eye that starts to sting.

There's no bravery medal for folks with cancer,
Though Congress should bestow one without pause,
Citing you for '*unflinching bravery in battle*',
And giving your life up fighting for the cause.

Trip to Cancer Land

I dreamt I sailed faraway,
To a place called Cancer Land.
Seeking a cure in an exotic place,
Of azure sea and golden sand.

In my dream I tossed to and fro,
Upon the shining sea.
Searching for a sorcerer,
Who holds the sacred key.

Sailing many a day and night,
'Neath stars of glittery gold.
While passing time poring over,
Journals new and old.

Vowing not to weaken,
Meager meals and rationed drink.
Fighting sleep in stormy weather,
Or risk drowning in the brink.

Finally, arrival in Cancer Land,
Comes at the break of day.
Many brethren came forward,
All willing to show me the way.

Rounding the bend, a sign read,
"*The Master of Oncology,*"
A man who mixes magical cures,
Using the art of wizardry.

Next, he sends you to a man,
Who wields the sharpest knives.
A third uses the moon's magical beams,
He claims save many lives.

The line stretched out for many miles,
So it was plain to see.
Many of my brethren were stricken,
By this miserable disease.

Despite these magic powers,
Vials of tincture and bottles of lotion.
They're governed by '*Feudal Drug Aristocrats*',
For every single potion.

The FDA's Feudal Lords,
Regulate all of Cancer Land.
Fiefdoms are required to adhere,
To its very strict demands.

The FDA has treasuries,
Stocked high with piles of gold.
It guards the 'trials' of jousters,
Who are so brave and bold.

All hope to endure the trials,
And make it to Phase Three.
But some will not endure,
While others simply flee.

You could get a one-way,
Pass to Cancer Land.
Where you'll be buried,
Beneath the golden sand.

Or down to the dungeon below,
Atop a '*DNR*' wagon.
Where you're greeted,
By a fire breathing dragon.

History says only the strong survive,
The rest get 'one to five'.
I believe that having faith and trust,
Also keeps you alive.

Those who leave wonder if,
They would return again if lured.
Will they need a coat of armor,
To protect them if they're cured?

Trudging their weary way back home,
To those they hold so dear.
They shake off bone deep weariness,
And try to bury the fear.

In the end, the weary travelers,
Accept what they already knew.
There's no real magic in Cancer Land,
The real 'cure' will find but a few.

The rest of us will be grateful to hold,
The hand of one we love.
And pray, with all that we hold dear,
For answers from above.

I awoke to face the day,
Shaking dreams from inside my head,
Gathered energy from the sun above,
And stretched atop my bed.

Thinking back to Cancer Land,
I was relieved it was a delusion.
Then dashed off to the Cancer Center,
For my weekly chemo infusion.

The Pink Ribbon Ball

It's an invitation to the Pink Ribbon Ball,
Oh my, the most glamorous one of all!
It can't be a mistake its addressed to me,
But I'm not part of that group in society.

The RSVP states I can bring a date,
I hope I find one before its too late.
My two rich step sisters will surely be there,
Dressed to the nines, while I have nothing to wear!

What will I do? My closet is practically bare!
Not a frock in sight, others have gowns to spare.
Just then, I see a flash of light under my bed,
Bending down to look, I think I've lost my head.

There's a great big box tied up with pink bows,
The logo is from a place that sells fancy clothes.
Where did this come from? Who put it there?
There's a note inside that I unfold with care.

"My dear, wear this to the Pink Ribbon Ball,
Please be home by midnight or lose it all.
I'm a guardian angel watching over you."
I have a benefactor that I never knew?

"Have a grand time in this pink confection,
Just be sure you follow my direction!"
"A limousine will come at eight o'clock
Wear these glass slippers with your frock."

"And don't worry about going alone,
I've arranged for a male chaperone."

"He will meet you at exactly half-past eight,
Wear purple ribbons in your hair and don't be late."
My poor head was spinning with every new detail,
I completed my response card and put it in the mail.

~ ~ ~ ~ ~

It's the night of the ball, I'm filled with anticipation,
I'm finally dressed up, despite slight exasperation.
It feels odd to be dressed in pink from head to toe,
This is for 'the cure', a little voice says "Don't go!

I've gotten so caught up with this entire metamorphosis,
Yet it seems out of place with my Stage IV metastasis.
That inner voice returned me to my reality for sure,
Should I be at a survivor's ball when I'm without a cure?

Feeling at an all time low I was ready to call it a night,
But a loud rapping at my window gave me quite a fright.
Turning, I saw a lovely vision, a woman dressed in white,
Floating in like mist from the sea, what a surreal sight!

She whisked me off to the ball before I could think twice,
The limo was plush and comfy, I had to admit this was nice.
Just as she said, my chaperone was waiting there,
His boutonnière matched the ribbons in my hair.
As I got close, I was so surprised, it was disarming,
It was my very own Oncologist, Dr. Peter Charming!

~ ~ ~ ~ ~

He was here to support me in this 'pink ball for the cure',
But I've heard the sponsors' motives weren't always pure.
The mission was to cure all with cancer in their breast,
But in time it became a 'big business' just like the rest.

Profiting from our cancer and selling everything in pink,
Not really curing, always celebrating, how do they think?
Big salaries for those at the top of their corporate tree,
Only two per cent of funds go to help people just like me.

No one will divulge the future for the pink community,
But thirty per cent of them will metastasize like me.
While we march to our doom, they have a pink parade,
Someone should call a halt to this pink charade.

~~~~~

Our arrival was announced, the entire group just stared,
Whispering through pink ruffles as royal trumpets blared.
I noticed them smile at each other, but not at me,
They fear that I'm Stage IV and sense my vulnerability.

The purple mixed with pink hair ribbons gave my status away,
They know I'm different from them and don't know what to say.
Not even my own step sisters bothered to welcome me,
They say I'm hopeless, I don't belong in a pure pink society.

Some say we carry an invisible cross on our shoulder,
We're headed to our funeral and won't get much older.
I know its not easy to make friends with someone like me,
It forces a tearful goodbye while facing your own mortality.

~~~~~

Where is the scientific passion to resolve our plight?
Why do they give up on us so easily without a fight?
Where is all the research money to prevent 'mets'?
Why is it that all we hear are delays and regrets?

The key to a cure for 'mets',
May lie within their reach.
"Please allocate the funds,
For Stage IV" I beseech.

~~~~~

Its clear I don't belong in this cheery pink palace,
Searching for a way to leave, I'm not one to be callous.
We danced round and round till I felt I would fall,
I saw it was nearing midnight on the big clock in the hall.

No time for goodbyes to Dr. PC, an escort so sweet and caring,
Scrambling to the street, I looked for the limo we'd be sharing.
It wasn't there . . . what should I do! Where is my angel in white?
Not to worry a soothing voice said as she lifted me in flight.

My pink satin slippers fell off as we flew out of sight,
Well, they never really belonged to me, try as I might.
We soared through the night till my house was in view,
We glided toward my open window and in we flew.

With two feet on the ground, I was relieved to be home,
Comfort is here and I swore never again to roam.
My angel asked "Is the grass greener on the other side?"
"No, it isn't," I said, with a note of foolish pride.

As I started to take off the pink gown and crawl into my bed,
I heard a knock at the door and answered it instead.
It was Dr. Charming with my pink satin slippers in hand,
"Return these", he said, "You don't need them to take a stand".

He understands my plight, he's full of empathy,
And he's just about the best doc in all Oncology.
"So, think you'll stay with Dr. Charming's treatment?"
"Yes" I said, "Remission is a pretty cool achievement!"

"I think I'm done here," my Guardian Angel said.
'Poof!' she was gone as she kissed me on the head.
I reflected on all that transpired this special day,
And a little wistful, I put the pink things away!

The End

Maybe Monday

One thing I know for certain,
My cancer's here to stay.
It never fails to warn me,
It always has its way!

Strong signals through my body,
Send an ominous warning.
Joint pain, backaches and fatigue,
Wake me up each morning.

I tell myself its all right,
That I will be okay.
But deep down I know,
Its worse than I can ever say.

Its demanding and always in charge,
I know I must obey.
Endure the tests, take the pills,
And pray it will go away.

This is my 'new normal' now,
I'm not a child at play.
Stage IV Breast Cancer,
Is a terrible price to pay.

Cancer knows no bounds,
Its aggressive and has its way.
Radiation, toxic drugs and surgery,
May not hold it at bay.

While grateful for remission,
I fervently pray.
For a miraculous cure,
Some future day.

Maybe next year, or next Spring,
Or in the month of May,
It may be next month, next week,
Or maybe even Monday.

Cancer Won't Beat Me Down

I fought, I battled with it,
I waged a God damn war.
I even wore pink ribbons,
Bought one in every store.

Took pills, shots and chemo,
The beast still wanted more.
I found a new clinical trial,
And came out with a smile.

Worked to keep my mind sound,
No, cancer won't beat me down.
Read all the latest longevity stats,
Cut out nasty sugars and fats.

Ate lots of fresh veggies and fruit,
Fish and poultry, red meat got the boot!
I stayed positive and strong,
So nothing would go wrong.

Fresh air and exercise every day,
Crosswords to help the memory stay.
Warm gloves at night for neuropathy,
Read the latest jokes to avoid apathy.

Tried all the wellness tips I found,
No, cancer won't beat me down.
Someday they'll put me in the ground,
But not because cancer beat me down.
Cancer may be the cause of my death,
But it was a full life till my last breath.

Cancerversary

Our society embraces celebrations,
Especially annual ones like a birthday.
Or that special wedding anniversary,
Family reunions, and Grandparents Day.

There's another to add to the calendar,
And its celebrants are so deserving.
It's the marking of cancer survival,
For a life that's worth preserving.

Each year gives us hope we live on,
To spend with our loved ones precious time.
The focus is on reaching to recovery,
Sheer faith fuels us for the climb.

A five-year survival was once the goal,
Now we're living longer and celebrating more.
Some have had a 25th Cancerversary,
I'd say that's worth fighting for.

So, let's light the candles,
And gather round to sing.
Another year added to a life,
T'will soften cancer's sting.

Glossary

Certs—Certifications are official documents that gives proof and details of something such as personal status, educational achievements, ownership, or authenticity; for physicians, it serves as evidence of current knowledge and/or competency to provide services in their specialty or area of practice.

Chemo—abbreviated form of chemotherapy; see below.

Chemotherapy—the use of chemical agents to treat diseases, infections, or other disorders, especially cancer

Dense Breast Tissue—the tissue is comprised of less fat and more connective tissue which appears white on a mammogram. Cancer also appears white on a mammogram, so tumors can be hidden behind the dense tissue. As a woman ages, the tissue becomes more fatty. Follow-up tests may be needed if the mammogram it questionable, such as an ultrasound or MRI.

DNR—do not resuscitate; a physician based on a patient's preference not to prolong life by emergency measures or artificial means.

Labile—readily or frequently undergoing chemical or physical change.

Mets—abbreviated form of metastasis; see below.

Metastasis—the spread of a cancer from the original tumor to other parts of the body by means of tiny clumps of cells transported by the blood or lymph.

MRI—Magnetic Resonance Imaging; an imaging technique that uses electromagnetic radiation to obtain images of the body's soft tissues, e.g. the brain and spinal cord. The body is subjected to a powerful magnetic field, allowing tiny signals from atomic nuclei to be detected and then processed and converted into images by a computer.

PET Scan—Positron Emission Tomography; an image of a bodily cross section that detects cancer, recurrent tumors, reveals the possibility of cancer metastasis (i.e., spreading to other sites), and determines if the therapy is working through a 3-D image.

Pheromes—chemical secreted by animals: a chemical compound, produced and secreted by an animal, that influences the behavior and development of other members of the same species.

Port—an implantable device usually placed under the skin of the chest wall for the purposed of long term intermittent infusions of drugs, chemotherapy or blood and blood products.

Progression—a gradual change or advancement from one state to another; in cancer, its recurrence of disease that will require further treatment of attention.

Scans—to obtain an image of internal organs with any of various devices, especially in order to make a diagnosis without the need for exploratory surgery, such as a bone scan or brain scan.

Stage 4 Breast Cancer—Metastatic or advanced breast cancer is the spread of breast cancer to non-adjacent parts of the body—most commonly to the bones, liver, lungs and/or brain. At present, the disease is not considered survivable.

Trials—Clinical Trials are a means of testing new drugs before placing them on the market; the drugs go through 4 distinct phases of highly regulated and supervised administration in test populations of animals, then humans who volunteer.

Über—exceptional of his or her kind; as in **Über**chef or **Über**model.